# Victorian and Edwardian
# CAMBRIDGE

*from old photographs*

*overleaf:* Market Hill, *c.* 1860

# Victorian and Edwardian
# CAMBRIDGE

*from old photographs*

*Introduction and commentaries by*

# F. A. REEVE

B. T. BATSFORD LTD
LONDON

First published 1971
This edition 1978
Text copyright © F. A. Reeve 1971
Printed in Great Britain by
The Anchor Press Ltd, Tiptree, Essex
for the Publishers
B. T. Batsford Ltd, 4 Fitzhardinge Street,
London W1H 0AH
ISBN 0 7134 0093 5

# CONTENTS

# ACKNOWLEDGMENTS

The Author and Publisher gratefully acknowledge the help given in making available some of the photographs by Miss Enid M. Porter, Curator of the Cambridge and County Folk Museum; Mr M. J. Petty of the City of Cambridge Public Library; Mr J. M. P. Farrar, Archivist of the Cambridgeshire and Isle of Ely County Council; Mr Arthur Halcrow of Trinity College Library and Mr Graham Pollard of the Cambridge Antiquarian Society.

The Cambridge and County Folk Museum for illustrations 3, 8, 32, 33, 37, 38, 43, 46, 47, 49–52, 55, 57, 69, 70, 72, 73, 75, 76, 82, 85, 86, 89, 92, 95, 104, 110, 113, 115–18, 120, 126, 128–33; The City of Cambridge Public Library: 9–13, 34, 35, 42, 47, 54, 56, 58, 62, 63, 80, 87, 90, 106, 108, 109, 114, 119, 121–4; Ramsey and Muspratt: 1, 2, 4–6, 15–17, 19–26, 29, 31, 39–41, 44–5, 48, 53, 60, 64–6, 78, 79, 81, 97; The Cambridge Antiquarian Society: 14, 18, 112; The Cambridge Evening News: 59, 77, 94, 96; Trinity College: 99, 100, 103, 127; The Records Office of the Cambridgeshire and Isle of Ely County Council: 27, 28, 30; Cambridge University Library: 84.

# INTRODUCTION

A press advertisement of 1884 stated that "Beard's Patent Daguerrotype, or Photographic Portraits, either plain or in colours, are taken daily (solely by the action of light) at the establishment, St Mary's Passage, Cambridge, where specimens may be seen". An editorial note expressed surprise that the beautiful and marvellous art of photographic portrait painting had not long since been introduced into Cambridge.

"People fancy that everything which is got in London is better than the same thing in the country; but, prima facie, a photographic portrait, taken by the action of light, will be more perfect when the plate is acted upon in the clear atmosphere of Cambridge than in the pea-soup affair which Londoners breathe."

The ancient commercial and domestic buildings of Cambridge never rivalled those in places like Bath, Chester, or York, yet some of the photographs in this book show that many were picturesque, and it is regrettable that so many have disappeared.

## THE EXPANSION OF THE TOWN

In 1841 there were 24,453 inhabitants. Some travellers arrived by coach even after the coming of the railway in 1845, and the stage coach between Cambridge and Bedford ran until 1894. Huge eight-horse waggons transported goods, and herds of oxen and sheep passed through the town on their way to market or to London.

The river trade was still important. Horses towed strings of barges, some with masts and sails, as far as Midsummer Common, then the bargees used stout poles called "spreads" along the Backs of the Colleges.

There were few streets more than a mile distant from the centre, barely a dozen houses south of Parker's Piece, and only a few in Romsey Town, New Chesterton, and Newnham. The Fitzwilliam Museum was unfinished, and there were not many buildings beyond the Shire House on Castle Hill. About one-sixth of the population lived in overcrowded tenements in courts and alleys behind the main streets, many without drainage or a water supply.

The Market Place was small until a spectacular fire in 1849 destroyed a large group of buildings near the east end of Great St Mary's Church, and it became possible to enlarge it to its present dimensions.

The university, too, was small. In 1849 there were 1,775 under-graduates, and only 355 matriculated in 1851. The area bounded by Free School Lane, Downing Street, and Corn Exchange Street was occupied by the Botanic Garden, and the building of the first scientific laboratories did not begin until 1863.

The Sturton Street district was developed in 1874, and by 1890, Romsey Town and Mill Road were much as they are today. The land on the east side of Hills Road beyond Hyde Park Corner was mainly meadows let to dairymen, butchers, and others. There was a great deal of building here in the late '80s and '90s, but still no streets or houses beyond the railway bridge.

In Chesterton, a large area known as the De Freville Estate came into the market, and many new roads of suburban villas were built. The growth of this district made a more direct and wider route neces-sary, and the obvious line for this was across Midsummer Common. Although the Common was in a rough state and little used, there was considerable opposition to the scheme, but the advocates of progress eventually prevailed, and the foundation stone of Victoria Bridge was laid in 1889.

The Cam Bridges Act of 1889 sanctioned a second bridge to be built nearer to Chesterton, and when Chesterton Urban District became part of the Borough in 1911, its residents were promised that the Chesterton Bridge would be provided by 1917. It was not, in fact, opened until 1971!

The new statutes of 1882 which allowed Fellows of Colleges to retain their Fellowships after marriage led to many large houses being built for the new households in the Grange Road district.

The Borough was jointly administered by the Town Council and by the Improvement Commissioners, the latter being responsible for paving, drainage, lighting, sewage disposal, plans for new buildings, and infectious diseases, but in 1889 the number of Councillors was increased, university representatives were included, and the Board of the Improvement Commissioners was abolished.

Nineteen main outfalls for the sewage of about 30,000 persons discharged into the river between Magdalene Bridge and Barnwell Pool, and in 1873 it was stated that four miles of the river were little better than a huge cesspool. A correspondant of the *Cambridge Review* said in 1888 that the stench was so bad that ''it seems a wonder that more boating men are not laid up with typhoid fever''. The new Council tackled the problem vigorously, and new sewers were constructed with the aid of a £150,000 loan.

The state of the river explains why men and boys bathed from Sheep's Green and Coe Fen. No costumes or trunks were worn, so no modest female approached the bathing-places. Ladies passing in boats unfurled parasols to shield their innocent eyes. In 1894 a ladder was provided above the iron bridge for the use of female bathers, and for several weeks letters in the press argued for and against the custom of nude bathing for men and boys. Two years later, an enclosure for women was opened, and Miss Hardy was appointed custodian at a salary of ten shillings a week.

## SPORT

The Town Rowing Club had been founded in 1863, but owing to the unsatisfactory state of the river and the popularity of cycling, town boat races were not firmly established until 1886. The first Head of the River Competition, in 1888, was won by the Albert Institute boat which had G. P. Hawkins, later to become mayor, at No. 4.

College rowing began in 1825, when St John's and Trinity formed boat clubs. The earliest boats were 40 feet long, with a beam of three to five feet. Mr Rutt, an old Cambridge boat-builder, stated that a sculling-boat was built by Mr Hughes, a Magdalene College undergraduate, and Dr Drosier of Caius, and launched near Jesus Locks, but "no boat-builder would then encourage such tomfoolery".

May Week was an important social event in Victorian and Edwardian times. People set off early in boats to secure good places to watch the bumping races, and there were wild scenes of confusion when everyone began to return after the last race. Until early in the twentieth century, Ditton Paddock belonged to the Rectory, and the Rector would hire two large marquees and provide teas with strawberries and cream. Sir Sydney Roberts has recorded that when he was an undergraduate, just before 1910, he was excited when a friend said that he would take him to the races in a motor car, and at Ditton Paddock he found about a dozen cars.

"Blues" were awarded only for rowing and cricket. Fenner let his private ground to the University Cricket Club in 1848, and large crowds watched the matches. The pavilion was always full of dons, including James Porter, the Master of Magdalene, with his dog, for which he had taken out life membership to quiet his conscience about breaking the rule that dogs were not admitted.

When cricket became popular, only Jesus College had its own ground, and undergraduates played on Parker's Piece. In the early 1860s, Cambridgeshire was one of the strongest county sides, and four town players, Hayward, Carpenter, Diver, and Tarrant, were in the All-England XI. A little later, Sir Jack Hobbs learned to play on Parker's Piece.

University men who played football found themselves in difficulties because they had come from schools with varying conceptions of the rules. A meeting in 1848 formulated rules for a game which was then a combination of soccer and rugger. Rules were again discussed in 1862, and soon afterwards the two games were established. The first Oxford and Cambridge rugby and soccer matches were held in 1872 and 1874.

In the '70s, lawn tennis had only recently been introduced, and golf was played on Coe Fen, and later on depressing links on Coldham's Common. Most reading men got their exercise by walking. Some, on Sundays, wearing caps and gowns, walked for five or six hours in the country. Professor G. M. Trevelyan, in his autobiography, records that he often walked 30 or 40 miles in a day, and with Geoffrey Winthrop Young he walked from Trinity College to Marble Arch in $12\frac{3}{4}$ hours.

## TRANSPORT

Visitors to Cambridge are often amazed to see so many bicycles. One well-known early cyclist was the Hon. Ian Keith Falconer who entered Trinity College in 1874, and the university had a "Bicycle Ground" at the corner of Madingley Road. Councillor C. A. E. Pollock rode a "penny farthing", and Mr Ralph Starr (twice mayor), possessed a "kangaroo", a bicycle with the front wheel about the same size as those of today, but with a small rear wheel.

The "safety bicycle", with solid tyres, arrived in 1886, but many of the older machines continued to be seen in the streets. Contemporary advertisements of dealers offered both "bicycles" and "safety bicycles" at prices between £3 and £12 or more. From 1896, Mr W. King and Mr H. H. Harper had a small cycle repair business in Sussex Street. They were interested spectators when, two years later, the Hon. C. S. Rolls, then an undergraduate, drove a motor cycle in the Corn Exchange. Mr King and a French mechanic drove a De Dion tricycle with a coach-built trailer attached, belonging to the Hon. C. S. Rolls, from Cambridge to Ely.

The firm built a number of "King" motor tricycles and bicycles and at the Motor Exhibition at the Crystal Palace in 1902 were awarded the Gold Medal for the "Best Motor Bicycle". The promotors regretted that as funds were low they could only give a bronze medal. W. King also gained silver medals in two 1,000-mile reliability trials, the first 100-mile Tri-Car Competition, and in September 1904 won the Motor Cycling Club Competition for an all-British-built motor cycle.

The Hon. C. S. Rolls owned the first car to appear in Cambridge, a 4 h.p. Peugeot. It was perhaps fortunate for the city that, unlike Morris at Oxford, King and Harper decided not to manufacture cars, but only to act as agents and repairers.

The Cambridge Street Tramways Company was formed in 1878, and an Act of 1879 authorised lines from the railway station to Christ's College and, via Lensfield Road and Trumpington Street, to Senate House Hill. In 1880, permission was given for a line from Hyde Park Corner, along East Road, to Fitzroy Street. The Tramways were mainly single track, with a few passing places, and at first there were two open-top double-deckers and four saloons. They travelled at a walking pace with a pleasant undulating motion.

At this time there were many autocratic and eccentric dons like Professor Newton (1829–1907), who disliked all innovations, and insisted on demonstrating his dislike by walking to his lectures in shepherd's plaid trousers, a silk gown, and an imposing top hat. When he reached the tramlines near Great St Mary's Church, he always walked between them in the middle of the road, and his appearance was so awesome and majestic that no horse tram driver ever sought to overtake him.

The trams faced competition in 1896 when the Cambridge Omnibus Company began to operate a horsebus service, and the company had to buy similar vehicles. A Motor Omnibus Company appeared in 1905, but had its licences withdrawn in 1906 after a number of accidents. In 1907 came the green "Ortona" buses, and so many people forsook the trams that the company had to be wound up in 1914. The last tramlines did not disappear from St Mary's Street until 1927.

# SOCIAL LIFE

Although a large proportion of Cambridge people worked as college servants or in shops catering almost exclusively for the undergraduates, at a higher level there were no social contacts between the university and the town. The Masters of Colleges and the Professors did not associate with anyone of lower social rank. M. G. Fawcett wrote: "My first glimpse of Cambridge was in 1867. It took me some time to apprehend the immense gulf which then separated the Heads of Colleges from persons of inferior university rank."

"The gulf flowed between the ladies as deep and strong as between members of the more exalted sex. The seats allotted to women in the University Church, Great St Mary's, were labelled 'For the Ladies of Heads of Houses', 'For the Ladies of Doctors of Divinity', 'For the Ladies of Professors', and so on, and socially the laws of precedence were most strictly observed, and controlled with the utmost vigour the movements of the ladies leaving the table after a dinner party, and on all other occasions."

Only a few people possessed their own carriage. The majority summoned a four-wheeler when necessary. Doctors, in top hats and frock coats, drove in Broughams. Hansom-cabs waited for hire on Senate House Hill, and yellow milk-carts, like Roman chariots, and lightly-built butchers' carts, raced over the cobbled streets. At a more leisurely pace came the carriers' carts bringing village women into Cambridge for shopping. As many as six women sat on each side, and some of the carts were open, while others had a canvas hood.

Before 1900, the waggons of the growers rumbled into the town at 4 a.m., and market stallholders and retailers would be up early to buy stock for the day. By 7 a.m. the stalls were ready for business, and they remained open until 10 p.m. There were about 30 stalls for butchers.

In 1910 the population was about 40,000, although Chesterton, Cherryhinton, and Trumpington were still outside the borough.

There were already traffic problems, particularly in Market Street and Petty Cury, and concern about the furious driving of the hansom-cab men, especially at the beginning of term. Many of their horses had formerly raced at Newmarket. The cabmen contrived to convey undergraduates' bicycles from the station by opening the apron-doors, and placing the cycle vertically on its rear wheel, where it was held by the passenger during the journey.

At a County Council meeting in 1907 it was moved that "The attention of the Chief Constable be directed to the large number of motor cars passing through the county at a greater speed than 20 M.P.H.".

Children played with hoops and marbles, and ran into the street when a barrel-organ man arrived, or the man who exchanged empty jam-jars for toy windmills. There were lamp-lighters with their long poles, and muffin men who rang a bell. College servants carrying on their head a large tray covered with green baize were a common sight in central streets, as they took lunch from college kitchens to under-graduates who were in lodgings. Later, a man with a large basket on wheels would collect the dirty crockery.

Since dressing for different occasions, and particularly for dinner, was the custom, there was much laundering to do. One family might wash for several colleges, collecting the laundry by hand-cart. It was hung out to dry on Laundress Green, Coe Fen, or Christ's Pieces. During the Long Vacation, carpets were taken to the Commons to be cleaned with long-handled beaters.

Beards and moustaches were common in the '50s and '60s, mous-taches only in about 1900. In the early '80s, the students wore Billy-cock hats, a kind of hard felt bowler, in winter, and straw hats with a band of ribbon in their college colours in summer. The custom of going hatless did not begin until after 1900. Before then, men boating on the river often wore black coats, stiff collars, and bowler hats. The girls had tight-bodiced, high-collared dresses which came down to the ground, and hats with a profusion of artificial fruit, flowers, and feathers. Up to about 1900, students still had to wear caps and gowns when walking in the country, and walking-sticks became popular early in the twentieth century.

At the end of the period depicted in this book, came the first manifestations of two things destined to play a major part in our life. At the Midsummer Fair in 1910, animated pictures were shown in a large tent. The chief attraction was a film of the funeral of King Edward VII, which had taken place a month earlier. Another film showed workers leaving the University Press, and there was great excitement when some of the audience recognised colleagues or friends.

Balloon ascents and parachute descents by the Spencer family were a feature of the Mammoth Shows held on August Bank Holidays on Jesus Green, and most Cambridge people saw an aeroplane for the first time when, in 1911, Second Lieutenant W. B. Rhodes Moorhouse landed a Blériot monoplane on Parker's Piece for a wager.

# EARLY CAMBRIDGE PHOTOGRAPHERS

In 1855 William Nichols of St Mary's Passage described himself as a "photographic portrait painter". W. Mayland in Market Street and E. Monson in Regent Street were listed in local directories as "photographic artists" by 1858. The first man to be described simply as a photographer was Arthur Nichols. This was in 1867, and his studio in Post Office Terrace was taken over later by several other photographers until the present day.

By 1881 J. E. Bliss was at these premises, and also in St Andrew's Street. He was succeeded by Valentine Blanchard by 1887, in partnership with Colin Lunn, who later was the sole proprietor. The name of J. Palmer Clarke is first mentioned in 1895 and it is probable that some of the photographs attributed to him were actually from plates that he acquired when he took over the existing premises. Palmer Clarke was at Post Office Terrace until 1933 and was succeeded by Ramsey and Muspratt in 1934.

Ralph Lord commenced at Market Hill between 1881 and 1883 and was followed in 1901 by Mason and Besebe. Stearn, a famous name in Cambridge photography, is first mentioned in 1874. Thomas Stearn senior had premises in King's Head Yard, off Magdalene Street, and Thomas Stearn junior was at 72 Bridge Street, where the business remained until recent years. Unfortunately, most of their old plates were destroyed when a bomb fell nearby.

Ralph Starr opened in Fitzroy Street between 1887 and 1891, and was joined by Rignall in 1904. Another early photographer was William Tams, butler to a Master of St John's College, who began to take photographs as a hobby, but later became a professional photographer and official photographer to the university.

# THE TOWN

1 (detail) Market Hill, *c.* 1860. One prominent figure is a police sergeant. Until the great fire of 1849 the market was an L-shaped area, with stalls extending into Peas Hill and Wheeler Street. Vendors of different commodities occupied defined parts of the market *(J. Palmer Clarke)*

**2** Market Hill, *c.* 1860, looking towards the east side, with the spire of Holy Trinity Church *(J. Palmer Clarke)*

3 Market Hill, *c.* 1900. The north side, showing two of the carrier's carts which transported people and goods to and from the surrounding villages. They were parked in the yards of inns in Bridge Street, King Street, and St Tibb's Row *(W. Tams)*

**4** Petty Cury, *c.* 1870, looking towards the Guildhall. Most of the buildings shown here no longer exist. In 1330 it was called Parva Cokeria, and later names were le Petitecurye, le Peticurie, and le Pety Cury. It is probable that part of the Market Hill was known as the Cury or Cook's Row, and that the street at a right angle to the Market Hill was called the Petty Cury to distinguish it from the larger Cury *(J. Palmer Clarke)*

**5** Petty Cury, *c.* 1870, looking towards Christ's College. Harry Johnson's newsagents and stationers business later removed to St Andrew's Street at the corner of Post Office Terrace *(J. Palmer Clarke)*

6 Petty Cury, *c.* 1870. A rear view of some of the picturesque old houses seen from the yard of the former Wrestlers' Inn *(J. Palmer Clarke)*

7 Petty Cury, *c.* 1910. The prominent building on the left was then the Head Post Office. In 1851 the office was removed from Green Street to new premises on the site of the old Brazen George Inn at 4 St Andrew's Street. When this building became too small, the new Post Office at the corner of Petty Cury replaced another notable relic of the stage coach era, the Wrestlers' Inn. This in turn became inadequate and a new building was erected in St Andrew's Street

8 Market Street, c. 1880. On the left are railings of Holy Trinity Church, then Macintosh's first shop. The firm later moved to the other side of the road, and the Henry Martyn Hall was built on the site

9 Slaughter House Lane, now Corn Exchange Street, 1870. On the left, the premises of Vinter, coal merchants, vacated in 1874. The old Corn Exchange was on St Andrew's Hill, formerly known as Hog Hill because the Hog and Horse Fair was held there

10 Wheeler Street, c. 1855. From left to right we see the Black Bear Inn, the entrance to its yard, then two shops occupied by J. Stanley, Scalemaker. Next came Parson's Court and the stables of Mortlock, the banker. These buildings were demolished when the Corn Exchange was built in 1876. Wheeler Street, formerly Short Butcher Row, was named after a basketmaker who lived there in the first half of the nineteenth century

11 (overleaf) Peas Hill, 1904. In 1570 it was called Peasemarket Hyll. The large room of the Guildhall is in the background. Additions to the Free Library were built on this corner site in 1916

12    Peas Hill, the Fish Market, *c.* 1900

13    St Bene't's Church, 1860. The north aisle had been re-built in 1853. The Anglo-Saxon tower, the oldest building in the county, was already standing when William the Conqueror landed. Thomas Hobson, the famous carrier, was buried in the chancel in 1632

14    Free School Lane, *c.* 1880. These buildings were re-placed when the old Engineering Laboratory was put up in 1893. The Perse Grammar School moved to Hills Road in 1890, and their original buildings were adapted to form part of this laboratory *(W. H. Hayles)*

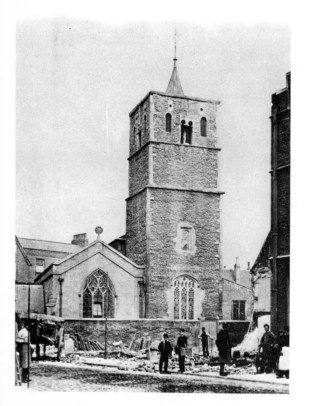

**15** Silver Street, 1890. It then had many picturesque old timbered houses, overhanging a thoroughfare only 13 feet wide. Six inns, the Wheatsheaf, the St Catharine's Wheel, the Black Lion, the Queen Adelaide, the Cock, and the Three Crowns were demolished to make way for the University Press, thus giving point to the quip that its rise to fame was built upon beer and the Bible. The Crown and Anchor, beside the bridge, was rebuilt and is now the Anchor *(J. Palmer Clarke)*

**16** *(opposite)* Trumpington Street, 1862. The buildings in the foreground have scarcely changed, although another storey was added to the shop at the corner of Silver Street in which the Neal family have carried on their tailoring business for a hundred years. In the distance are the old buildings demolished for Sir G. G. Scott's Chetwynd Building of 1870. The church was dedicated to St Botolph, the East Anglican patron saint of travellers, because it adjoined the Trumpington Gate, one of the limits of the ancient town. James Essex, a native of Cambridge who was a notable eighteenth-century architect, is buried in the churchyard. The trees stood in front of St Catharine's College *(J. Palmer Clarke)*

**17** Trumpington Street, 1862, before Emmanuel Congregational Church had been built. On the left, at the corner of Pembroke Street, was Hall's bookshop *(J. Palmer Clarke)*

18  Downing Street, *c*. 1890. The wall on the left was the boundary of the grounds of Downing College. The buildings now on this site, the Sedgwick Museum of Geology and the former Squire Law Library, were opened by King Edward VII and Queen Alexandra in 1904. On the right, the premises of Whitmore & Co., wine merchants, established in 1770, still exist, but the building erected for the Professor of Anatomy in the angle of Downing Street and St Andrew's Hill in 1832–33 was demolished in 1900

19  St Andrew's Street, *c*. 1860. From a first floor window of the second building on the left, then a university lodging house, I watched a suffragette procession in about 1912 *(J. Palmer Clarke)*

**20**   The Corner of Christ's Lane, *c.* 1860. The building depicted here was rebuilt and in recent times was occupied by Roe's antiques shop. Bradwell's Court now occupies the site, and Christ's Lane has disappeared *(J. Palmer Clarke)*

21   The Fountain public house, the Police Station, the Spinning House, and the Baptist Chapel, 1898. The Spinning House was founded in 1628 in property given by Thomas Hobson. Governed by trustees appointed by the town and the university, it was a workhouse for the poor where spinning was done until early in the nineteenth century. It was also a "house of correction for unruly and stubborn rogues". Eventually it served mainly as a prison for prostitutes who could be arrested by the Proctors and tried in the Vice-Chancellor's court. Innocent girls were sometimes apprehended and condemned, and the powers possessed by the university caused much bitterness in the town. In 1891 a wrongful arrest led to national protests and the university had to surrender its powers to the town. The Spinning House was demolished in 1901 *(J. Palmer Clarke)*

22   Emmanuel Street, 1913. A row of old shops and houses occupied the north side of Emmanuel Street. They were demolished for the North Court of Emmanuel College, opened in 1914. When one considers the amount of traffic carried by this street today, it is surprising to recall that between 1902 and 1907 the College proposed that it should be closed. Negotiations with the Corporation broke down, and a subway connects the North Court with the remainder of the College *(J. Palmer Clarke)*

23   *(opposite)* Trinity Street, 1878. The buildings of Caius College on the left were demolished when Waterhouse rebuilt Tree Court. St Michael's Church appears to be in a bad state of repair, and just beyond, St Michael's Court had not yet been built *(J. Palmer Clarke)*

**24** Trinity Street, *c.* 1890, with Tomlin's bookshop in the left foreground. The words "Discount Bookseller" on the sign recall the days before the Net Book Agreement of 1899, when books were sold at a discount. The building on the right has been rebuilt for the National Provincial Bank *(J. Palmer Clarke)*

**25** *(opposite)* All Saints Church, 1865, demolished and rebuilt in Jesus Lane. The tower, protruding over the foot-walk, made the street very narrow at this point *(J. Palmer Clarke)*

26  All Saints Passage, 1870. It was formerly called Dolphin Passage after a famous inn. The site of the Divinity School was occupied by stables and by chambers for scholars of St John's College not on the foundation, and therefore called the Pensionary. The Selwyn Divinity School was completed in 1879 at the joint cost of the university and of the Reverend Wm. Selwyn, B.D., Lady Margaret Professor of Divinity (1855–75), who contributed nearly £9,000. The buildings on the extreme right still remain (J. Palmer Clarke)

27  Sidney Street, 1870. The clock was on the shop of Wehrle, jewellers, who ceased trading (from a different address) in 1970. The firm of Gallyon, gunsmiths, now in Bridge Street, is probably the oldest business in the city still carried on under the original name. Established in Green Street in 1784, it moved to Sidney Street in 1832

28  Bridge Street, 1910. The ancient buildings on the left were demolished in 1939 when new ones were put up for St John's College. On the right are the high railings surrounding the churchyard of St Sepulchre's, more commonly called the Round Church. Until 1841 the church was screened by trees and thick buttressed walls about 18 feet high

**29** Magdalene Street, 1860. All of the buildings on the left have been preserved, but those to the right and left of the main frontage of Magdalene College have disappeared. Salmon's Lane separated the college and a number of small houses, those abutting on the river being mostly ale-houses *(J. Palmer Clarke)*

**30** Magdalene Street, 1904, looking from the corner of Northampton Street towards the bridge. All of the buildings on the right still exist, but those opposite were demolished in 1912. There were about twelve small houses, the *Swans* and the *King's Head* alehouses and the brewery of Mann and Wootten, also two courts

**31** Chesterton Lane and Magdalene Street Corner, 1911, just before these old buildings were demolished and re-placed mainly by a wall and a spacious hall added by Dr Benson in 1912 for concerts and college club meetings *(J. Palmer Clarke)*

**32** Chesterton Lane, 1896. The old cottages were pulled down in 1911. In the background is the woodyard which adjoined the White Horse Inn, now the Folk Museum, making a very narrow entrance to Northampton Street *(W. Tams)*

**33** Chesterton Road, 1896, with a London and North Western Railway delivery van and a two-horse omnibus. This part of the road remains unchanged *(W. Tams)*

34 Old St Giles Church, 1875, as demolition was beginning after the completion of the new church seen in the background. The clock was until 1817 in the clock-house between the N.E. turret and the first northern buttress of King's College Chapel. It was removed to the old St Giles Church, and was placed in its present position when the new church was built

35 Queen's Road, *c.* 1900. Today it is crowded with traffic *(Jarrolds)*

**36** Garret Hostel Lane, *c.* 1890. Only the children show that this is not a recent view. The Hostel was incorporated in the foundation of Trinity College

**37** The Town Gaol, *c.* 1870. Erected in 1827 in Gonville Place, overlooking Parker's Piece, it contained eight day-rooms and eight yards and could accommodate forty-seven criminals. The debt incurred by the erection of this spacious building was not paid off until 1847. It was pulled down in 1878, and prisoners were henceforth sent to the county gaol

38   The Old Trumpington Windmill, *c.* 1880. Built in 1812, it stood on the north side of Long
Road, near the junction with Trumpington Road. It ceased working in 1887 and a year later was
sold to Mr John Piele, Master of Christ's College. When he failed to find a tenant, he had it pulled
down. The photograph was taken by Ralph Lord and won a contemporary photographic competition

# INNS

**39**  Ye Olde Castel Hotel, St Andrew's Street, *c.* 1890, was one of the oldest inns in Cambridge, and had a most attractive exterior. It was established before 1243, and was reconstructed *c.* 1620. Extensive additions were made in 1891. Severely damaged by fire in 1934, it was demolished to make way for the Regal Cinema *(J. Palmer Clarke)*

**40** The Castle Inn, Guildhall Street, 1878. It was pulled down to provide a site for the old police court. Guildhall Street was formerly Butcher Row *(J. Palmer Clarke)*

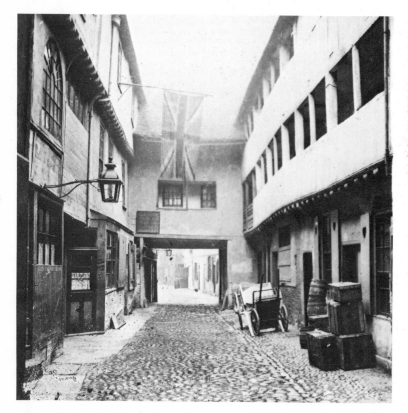

**41** The Falcon Inn, Petty Cury, *c.* 1890. Falcon Lane is the yard of the Falcon Inn which was one of the most important in the town. Mentioned in the borough accounts for 1516 and 1528, it had a fifty-foot frontage on Petty Cury, and timber buildings with open galleries on the first and second floors from which the quality watched dramatic performances being given in the yard. The galleries on the left were destroyed to form a large reception room. Queen Mary saw "a play at the Fawcon Inn" in 1557 *(J. Palmer Clarke)*

42 The Wrestlers' Inn, 1880. Situated on the site of the old Head Post Office at the corner of Petty Cury, it was a very picturesque building of the early part of the seventeenth century. So late as 1749 a "Great Muscovy Bear" was baited here, and it was announced that "The whole Entertainment will Conclude with a Scene worthy Observations of the curious".

43 The Nelson and True Blue Public House, Sidney Street, c. 1910. It has such a rural appearance that one would not suppose that it formed part of the site of the Dorothy supermarket, restaurant, and ballroom. It was a favourite meeting place for carriers. Next door, G. Barnes, the crack shot of the Volunteers, had a small baker's shop. Ranjitsinhji lodged there

**44** *(opposite)* The Hoop Hotel, Bridge Street, *c.* 1870. More stage coaches arrived at or departed from it than from any other inn. Wordsworth, describing his arrival in Cambridge in 1787 in "The Prelude" wrote:

*Onward we drove beneath the Castle, caught While crossing Magdalene Bridge, a glimpse of Cam;*

*And at the Hoop alighted, famous inn.*

Three hundred electors dined there in 1834 to celebrate the re-election of the Rt. Hon. Thomas Spring Rice to Parliament. While owned by the Ekin family, premises used by the Union Society from 1831–50 and later by the Amateur Dramatic Club were built at the rear. In 1857 the site was acquired by the New Music Hall and Public Rooms Company, Cambridge, Ltd., which proposed to erect a concert hall to seat about two thousand persons, a ballroom, lecture rooms, public baths, an hotel, and a restaurant, but the scheme was abandoned in the following year *(J. Palmer Clarke)*

**45** The Bird-Bolt Hotel, St Andrew's Street, *c.* 1870. This stood at the corner of Downing Street, and in medieval times belonged to St John's Hospital, and later to St John's College. It was formerly called The Hanging Burbolt or the Burbolt. In *c.* 1440 a brydbolt or burdebolt was a kind of blunt-headed arrow used for shooting birds *(J. Palmer Clarke)*

**46** The White Horse Inn, Castle Street, *c.* 1900. Built in 1423 as a farmhouse, it is now the home of the Folk Museum. When this photograph was taken, Jenkin's fish shop occupied part of the premises. A woodyard at the side of the inn extended over part of Northampton Street until about 1910

**47** The Three Tuns, 1903. Better known as Whyman's Inn, it stood at the top of Castle Street. It was built early in the seventeenth century, and was one of the lairs of Dick Turpin, the famous highwayman. It was from this inn that Elizabeth Woodcock set out upon her adventurous journey home to Impington, when she fell from her horse into a snowdrift and was buried for eight days before she was discovered, severely frostbitten but still alive. The Three Tuns was pulled down in 1936

**48** *(overleaf)* The Half Moon Inn at the corner of Little St Mary's Lane and Trumpington Street, 1872. Emmanuel Congregational Church was built on the site in 1875 *(J. Palmer Clarke)*

49  Mr Arthur Deck standing in front of his chemist's shop at 9 King's Parade,
1872. The firm was founded by his namesake on the Market Hill before 1800,
and he was succeeded by his brother in 1815, when the business was removed
to King's Parade. Isaiah Deck was called Guy Fawkes by his friends because he
had a high reputation as a pyrotechnist and organised firework displays for
special occasions. When he died in 1853 he was succeeded by his son Arthur
who served the town as a councillor and alderman for nearly fifty years.
Among famous customers were H.R.H. the Prince of Wales (later King Edward
VII), the Prince Consort, and the Duke of Clarence.

An advertisement in the *Cambridge Chronicle* in 1806 reads:

*A. Deck, Chemist*

*Market-Place, Cambridge*

*has received a fresh supply of Iceland Moss and Chocolate so highly recommended
for its medicinal and nutritive properties, for inveterate Coughs, Colds, Con-
sumptions and Pulmonic Complaints.*

*The Egyptian Furniture Paste.*

*Japan Varnish for beautifying Fronts of Stoves.*

*Refined Lemon Juice for instantly making Punch, Negus, Lemonade, etc.*

For three generations, until 1914, the Deck family fired rockets to welcome
the New Year from the open space before the college entrance opposite

# SHOPS

50   Hutt, Basket Maker, c. 1890. This picturesque shop stood on the west side of Peas Hill. The smaller central sign reads:
HUTT
BASKET, BRUSH
MEASURE, SIEVE &
GENERAL TURNERY WAREHOUSE.
FANS. SEEDLOPS.
In more recent times the business belonged to Shrive

**51** Macintosh, Market Hill, *c.* 1890. William Macintosh founded his coppersmith's business in 1814, and his son Alexander added the ironmongery side. In 1884 the firm moved from 23 Market Street to 14 Market Hill when the business of Edward Beales was purchased. An iron business on this site was taken over in 1688 by Finch, who came from Dudley, and throughout the eighteenth century they purchased the iron that they needed from relatives in Dudley or Birmingham. Their foundry, on the site of St John's College Lodge and later in Thompson's Lane, cast Magdalene Bridge and the former Silver Street Bridge

**52** Barrett's, *c.* 1910. Then situated on Market Hill, it was the leading china shop

**53** *(opposite)* Miller's Music Warehouse, Sidney Street, *c.* 1900. At this time the firm built, tuned, and repaired organs in many churches in Cambridgeshire and even far-distant places. A part of their premises going through to Hobson Street had previously been occupied by Hunnybun, Carriage Builders. Mr A. H. Miller was organist at Great St Mary's Church *(Ramsey and Muspratt)*

**54** *(opposite)* Sebley's Tea, Coffee, and Dining Rooms in Bridge Street, *c.* 1900. Formerly the *Barley Mow*, it was a well-known eating-house famous for its hams *(J. G. Simpson)*

**55** Ellis Merry's ambulance, much used by local doctors to move patients to and from nursing homes. Ellis Merry stands at the head of the stretcher. He had the first motor hearse in Cambridge, and in addition to his undertaking business kept a livery stable and riding school

**56** An Onion Seller

**57** Cambridge Yard Butter-Seller, *c.* 1900. The custom of selling butter in 3-foot lengths was peculiar to Cambridge. A pound of butter was weighed and then rolled into a yard in length between two boards. University officials have an archaic cylinder of sheet iron, a yard long and an inch in diameter, which was used to test the dimensions of every roll of butter sold in the town. ''Yard Butter'' was still sold on the market stall of Mr J. Hopkins of Stretham until the custom died out during the early years of the 1914–18 war on the introduction of rationing

**58** A Fish Curer, Bridge Street, *c.* 1890

**59**    The Milk Float of H. Doggett, *c.* 1910

**60**  Senate House Hill and the west side of Trinity Street, *c.* 1860. The houses were acquired by Caius College in 1782, and partly converted into rooms for students in 1854. These buildings were demolished when Waterhouse rebuilt Tree Court in 1868–70 *(J. Palmer Clarke)*

# THE UNIVERSITY

**61**   Senate House Hill, *c.* 1900, with the hansom-cab rank

62 St John's College, 1863. The old chapel, seen on the left, was pulled down in 1869 after the completion of the new chapel, 1863–69. St John's Lane, closed in 1862, ran by the side of the college and here stood the infirmary of the old Hospital of St John which had been adapted for college rooms and was known as "The Labyrinth".

One day the Master was in one of these rooms, which had heavy iron bars across the windows, when he saw a man misbehaving in the lane. He called out, "What are you doing there?" and the man replied, "You aren't there for your good deeds". The Master said "Be off with you, man", and the man replied, "Ah, I can go where I like, but you can't get out", evidently thinking that the man behind the barred window was in prison

63 St John's College, the Old and New Chapels, 1869

**64** St John's Street, 1865. All Saints Church was then being demolished. Two years earlier, in 1863, St John's College had begun to destroy half of First Court to make room for an enlarged Hall and a new Chapel. The latter building may be seen rising in the centre background *(J. Palmer Clarke)*

**65** The Bakery of St John's College, 1877, on part of the site later occupied by the Divinity Schools. In former times, every college brewed its own ale and many baked their own bread *(J. Palmer Clarke)*

**66**  Gonville and Caius College, the Old Court, *c.* 1860. It was demolished when Waterhouse built Tree Court in 1870 (*J. Palmer Clarke*)

**67**  The First Women Students, 1870, when they occupied a house at Hitchin and received instruction from five Cambridge lecturers. One wing and a small Hall were built at Girton in 1873. A few resident female dons taught in the mornings, and male lecturers in the afternoons. Carriages were provided for students going to lectures in the town.

Cans of hot water were brought to the rooms at 7 a.m., breakfast was at 8.15, lunch from 12 until 3. Afternoon tea-trays were taken to all rooms at 4 p.m. and dinner was at 6 p.m. The rules about male visitors were strict: "No gentlemen, however nearly related, except parents and guardians"

**68**  Girton College Fire Brigade, 1887

**69**  A Student's Room at Newnham College, 1894. A Girton student of 1882 wrote that rooms had an abundance of pictures, photographs, and china ornaments, large stands for plants, peacock feathers and mantel-cloths

**70** Newnham College Students, 1897. Five students occupied a house in Regent Street in 1871. Merton Hall was then leased until Old Hall was opened in 1875. Catherine Durring Holt wrote in *Letters from Newnham College,* 1889–92 that "I have been having such a dissipated time of it these last few days. Each evening a cocoa party"

72  Vote on the Admission of Women to Degrees, 21st May, 1897. Undergraduates invading the rooms above Bacon's tobacco shop. William Bacon
founded his business at 63 Sidney Street, and Charles Darwin lodged in rooms
above the shop. Bacon moved to the corner of Rose Crescent soon after 1828.

Old ledgers record the names of many famous customers, including Edward
FitzGerald, H.R.H. The Prince of Wales (later King Edward VII), Tennyson,
Charles Kingsley, and Samuel Butler. Another renowned customer, Charles
Stuart Calverley, came up to Christ's College in 1835 and his "Ode to Tobacco"
is engraved on a bronze plaque affixed to a wall of the shop

71  (opposite) Degrees for Women. The scene on Senate House Hill, 1897, while voting was taking place to decide
whether degrees should be awarded to women. A female figure on a bicycle was suspended from an upper window
of Macmillan and Bowes, booksellers

73   Edward, Prince of Wales, taking his Honorary Degree, 1892 *(Scott and Wilkinson)*

74   Cambridge University Constables, popularly known as Bulldogs, 1896

75   A Mock Funeral Procession, *c.* 1910, passing the Globe public house, Hills Road. Undergraduates who were sent down from the university after a serious offence were given a mock funeral on their way to the railway station

76   The Proclamation of King George V, 1910, by the university from the steps of the Senate House

**77**  A College Bedmaker, *c.* 1920. When female bedmakers were first employed, they were always elderly, and the statutes of one college said that they must be "of horrible appearance". In Victorian times no unmarried women could be employed. The lady seen here is Mrs C. E. Binder. Her "gentlemen", as she always referred to them, never forgot her and wrote to her from all corners of the world

# THE RIVER

78 Bullen's Boatyard and Fisher Lane viewed from Magdalene Bridge, *c.* 1880. Bargees lodged in these houses which were conveniently close to Quayside. W. Childs, a shoeing smith, lived at No. 7, but had his forge in Northampton Street. Mr Prime, who lived in Mill Lane and managed the Anchor boatyard, is said to have brought the first punt to Cambridge after he had seen them used for racing at Henley *(J. Palmer Clarke)*

79 *(overleaf)* The Conservators of the River Cam, 1887, about to set off from Jesus Locks for an inspection of the river. The footbridge, built in about 1851, was condemned in 1892. Chesterton Road looks bare without the trees, although some, seen here, had just been planted to celebrate Queen Victoria's Jubilee.

The River Cam Navigation Act, 1851, placed the river between King's Mill and Clayhithe under the care of eleven Conservators, five from the county, three from the university, and three from the Town Council *(J. Palmer Clarke)*

**80** The King's and Bishop's Mills, *c.* 1890. From at least Conquest times, the King's Mill built by Sheriff Picot, and the Bishop's Mill belonging to the Abbot of Ely, occupied this site. At one time one could walk from the mills to Queens' College Bridge on barges waiting to be unloaded. Bishop's Mill was acquired by John Anderson in 1777, and from his descendants it passed, together with the King's Mill, to the Nutter family. In 1842 James Nutter sold them to Foster, the well-known Cambridge milling and banking family. These mills were pulled down in 1928

**81** William Bates, a famous character, who had one of the five ferries which afforded passage over the river to Chesterton, *c.* 1880. They were the Pike and Eel, Dant's, the Fort St George, the Horse Grind, and one from Jesus Green to the garden of the New Spring. This continued for some years after Victoria Bridge was opened in 1890 (*J. Palmer Clarke*)

**82** The Horse Grind Ferry between Chesterton and Stourbridge Common, *c.* 1900. Two ferries afforded passage for a horse and cart as well as for pedestrians. ''Old Alf'' worked his ungainly craft for thirty-four years before it was replaced by a footbridge in 1935

**83** Another Ferry at Chesterton, *c.* 1880

**84** *(previous page)* Spectators at the May Boat Races, *c.* 1905. In 1904 a local newspaper complained about the entire absence of any order on the river and the number of accidents that occurred in consequence as boats returned after the races. "A more haphazard and disorderly scene can hardly be imagined than was presented each night of the 'Mays' at the conclusion of the racing. Steam launches, panting, wheezing and hooting like asthmatical motor cars, huge barges fitted up as houseboats and drawn by horses, ferryboats with the dangerous chains and innumerable small craft were all striving to make their way along the river at one and the same time and with an absence of order that could only end in disaster"

**85** Newnham Mill Pool, *c.* 1900. Mott's cows forded the river four times a day when going between Sheep's Green and the cowshed where they were milked. The *Jolly Millers* public house of 1490 on the left had been rebuilt in 1903. The front of the seventeenth-century brewery in the background was demolished in 1902 when the Corporation widened the road. The building was converted into a dwelling called The Malting House, and two of the outhouses were taken down.

In 1912 the remains of the malting used to store grain were converted into a small hall with two galleries and a stage. Many concerts and meetings have been held there, including a lecture by Albert Schweitzer on Bach

# TRANSPORT

**86** *The Eagle*, the only locomotive to be built in Cambridge. It was a small single-tank engine constructed at Headly Bros. foundry in Mill Road in 1849. It ran on the old Norfolk Railway

**87** *(overleaf)* The Cambridge, Oxford and London Coach outside the Bull Hotel, 1879. Mr Moyes, the owner of the hotel, is in the foreground *(Scott and Wilkinson)*

**88**  The Cambridge Street Tramways Company ran services from 1880 until 1914. In this picture, car number 8 waits near the railway station. In September 1882 a gentleman wrote to the press to say that as an old Cambridge man visiting Alma Mater after an interval of more than forty years, he was much distressed to see how on Saturdays the trams were overladen, and the one poor horse made to draw a load which requires two

89    Car Number 5 waits near the Senate House as a university procession is approaching

90 A horsebus. Mr Henry Willis with one of the horsebuses of the Cambridge Omnibus Company which began to operate in 1896. The Tramways Company fought this competition by buying some similar vehicles

91 The Cambridge Motor Omnibus Company commenced to operate in 1905, but had their licences withdrawn in 1906 after a number of accidents. Here we see one of their vehicles on Market Hill. The gentleman in the top hat was Alderman P. J. Squires

92   A "Special Trip". One of the towers of Ely Cathedral is visible in the
background *(Starr and Rignall,* 1906*)*

93   A Horse Tram about to pass a successful rival. In 1907 Mr Walford of Abergavenny obtained licences to run his
green "Ortona" buses. He began with three omnibuses licensed to carry sixteen passengers which ran from the Railway Station to the Post Office

**94**    The First Electric Brougham in Cambridge. The Reverend Stephen Parkinson, D.D., F.R.S., Praelector of St John's College, seated in the vehicle in front of The Hermitage, Silver Street. The house had been built by Mr S. P. Beales, the leading partner of Messrs Beales, corn and coal merchants, whose carts made deliveries over a wide area. The firm had a quay, granary, and warehouse in the vicinity, and did a large trade at the port of Lynn. The building now forms part of Darwin College

**95**  A Matthew & Son Delivery Van, *c.* 1910. The firm then had a large grocery business in Trinity Street

**96**  *(overleaf)* The Wheatsheaf (Castle Hill) Ladies Outing Club about to set out for a charabanc excursion, 1924 *(Ramsey and Muspratt)*

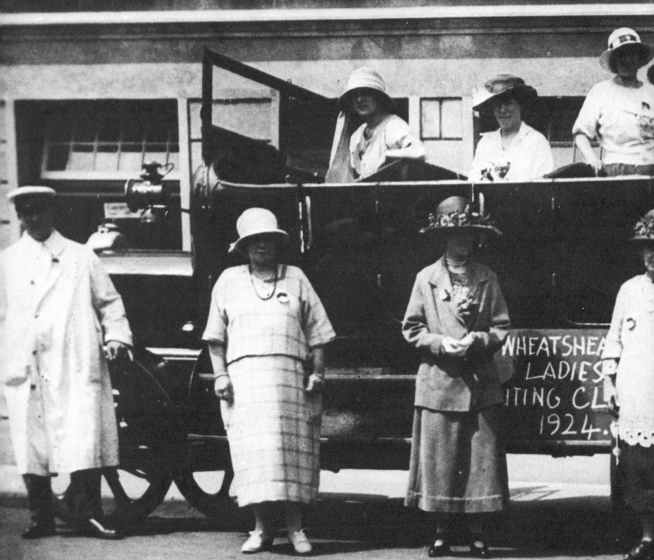

**97** The Garage of the University Arms Hotel, 1905, when motor cars were ousting carriages. On the right is a horse-bus used to take hotel guests to and from the railway station *(Ramsey and Muspratt)*

# SPORT

**98** Two Cambridge Cricketers, Tom Hayward, uncle of the great Surrey batsman, and Bob Carpenter, who in the 1860s, with Richard Daft of Nottinghamshire, were first choice for the All-England sides. Hayward was born in 1835 and died in the 1870s, and Richard Daft said that "Hayward was one of the most beautiful players to look at that ever went to the wicket. . . . He could hit brilliantly all round, and his defence was wonderful".

Robert Carpenter, born at Mill Road in 1830, became famous as the greatest exponent of back play, a punisher of slow bowling, and one of the best fielders at point ever seen

**99**   Trinity College Head of the River Crew, 1870. They defeated St John's and confirmed this victory by winning the Granta Challenge Cup at King's Lynn by four lengths

**100**   First Trinity Second Boat Crew, May 1888. They made a bump every night, always before reaching Grassy Corner

**101** Albert Institute Head of the River Crew, 1888. W. Camps (bow), A. Cox (2), C. King (3), G. P. Hawkins (4), Walter Betts (5), G. Curtis (6), William Betts (7), E. Fordham (stroke), H. Turner (cox). G. P. Hawkins founded the well-known bakery and catering firm and became mayor

**102** Rovers Cycling Club, 1891

**103** College Servants Cricketers on Trinity Old Field, 1892. Included in this group are Mr Anable ("Baths Man"), Mr Coote (father of Sam Coote who was the college plumber), Mr A. Hunt (champion county mile runner), Mr Marshall (manager of the Pitt Club and founder of the motor firm), and Mr Nichols (butcher in Guildhall Street who supplied meat to the college). The original photograph belonged to the publican of the *Pike and Eel*, who collected pig food from Trinity College kitchens

**104** Newnham College Hockey XI, 1897. They played on a secluded pitch, and although skirts reached almost to the ground, a man brought by a visiting team at Girton as an umpire was requested to leave before the game commenced

**105** Liberal Club Athletic Sports at Fenner's in the late '90s. The famous cricketer Ranjitsinhji is the sixth from the left in the middle row, behind the Reverend and Mrs Austin Leigh in the centre

# SPECIAL OCCASIONS

106  The Lion Hotel, Petty Cury, during the County Election, 1874. The
*Cambridge Independent Press* reported on the 3rd October, 1874, that "Mr
Powell has left his mark behind in this county. Almost every dead wall, barn
and Tory public-house, proclaims the name of Francis Sharp Powell, the
'chosen Conservative Candidate'. The well-known Hotel, *The Lion*, at Cambridge, was plastered from roof to basement with Mr Powell's memorable
address, and other placards"

**107**  The Footbridge at Jesus Locks after the great storm in August, 1879, when floods reached to within fifty yards of Maids' Causeway. More than three inches of rain fell in six hours, and the river rose eight feet in two or three hours. "The lightning and thunder", says a contemporary record, "were awful in grandeur, and the downpour of rain and hail terrible. . . . Trees were torn up, mills wrecked, cattle were killed in the field and more died from drowning; farms were set on fire by the electric fluid and churches were stricken"

**108**  The Diamond Jubilee, 22nd June, 1897. The decorations in Petty Cury *(Scott & Wilkinson)*

**109**  *(opposite)* The Relief of Mafeking Bonfire, 1900. The undergraduates had another huge unofficial bonfire on the Market Hill, tearing down shutters and fences to feed the flames. The defender of Mafeking was Baden-Powell, the founder of the Boy Scout Movement

110 Reception in the Guildhall for men who had returned from the Boer War, 1902

111 The Sultan of Zanzibar Hoax, 1905. The undergraduates who took part in this famous hoax were, from left to right, Adrian Stephen, Bowen Colthurst, Horace Cole, Leland Buxton, and "Drummer" Howard. They were made up at a theatrical costumiers in London, then sent a telegram to the mayor to announce their visit. They were met at the station by the Town Clerk, and driven in a carriage to the Guildhall, where they were received by the mayor. They visited a charity bazaar, were shown the principal colleges, and eventually conducted back to the station by the Town Clerk

**112** May Day Garlands, 1904. The girls are walking on the path in the Backs running beside Queen's Road *(W. H. Hayles)*

**113**   Coronation of King Edward VII, 1902. The procession entering Market Street. Note the horse-drawn fire engine
*(R. H. Lord)*

# THE VOLUNTEERS

**114**  Cambridge University Rifle Volunteers on the lawn of King's College, *c.* 1859. On 30th April, 1859, some Cambridge men suggested to the mayor and to the university that a Rifle Club should be formed to enable men to acquire skill in shooting and to encourage those who might be willing to serve their country in time of need. The Home Secretary welcomed the proposal, and the Cambridge Rifle Club was formed. On the 9th May, Tennyson's poem "Riflemen, form!" appeared in *The Times*, and many other clubs were established in other parts of the country.

In Cambridge, two Corps were formed, "The Cambridge University Rifle Volunteers" and "The First Cambridgeshire Volunteer Rifles". The official title of the university Corps became "The Third Cambridge Rifle Volunteers" and they wore a uniform of light grey. In 1887 the Corps became the "Fourth (Cambridge University) Volunteer Battalion of the Suffolk Regiment".

Later, a third Corps was raised among the residents of the town, chiefly from members of the Working-men's College, and called "The Eighth Cambridgeshire Rifle Volunteers". These three Corps used a range on Mill Road

115    The Sixth Cambridgeshire Volunteer Rifle Corps in camp, 1876

# THE WORKHOUSE

**116** The Master's Drawing Room, *c.* 1880. In the early years of the nine-teenth century, reformers attempted to classify the paupers of Cambridge by housing the young, the aged, and the able-bodied in six of the old parish workhouses. This policy was abandoned when a general mixed workhouse was built in Mill Road in 1838.

Mr Luke Hosegood, the Master, received a testimonial for "his prompt and meritorious action in rescuing some inmates from a fire that happened in the Infirmary of the Cambridge Union Workhouse at 3 a.m. on the 8th April, 1883". He died in 1924

117    The Men's Infirmary, with the Matron, Mrs Hosegood, and a nurse

118    The Aged Women's Day-Room, with the Matron

# PEOPLE

**119** Three Stage-Coach Drivers, *c.* 1850, who had to retire after the coming of the railway. At the foot of the photograph is a drawing of "The Usurper"

**120** Charles Rowell, a world champion long distance runner, was born at Chesterton in 1851. He often ran to Ely before breakfast and once ran ten miles in an hour. At Madison Square Gardens in 1879 he defeated the reigning champion in a 500-mile race lasting for six days, to gain the world championship silver belt, with a gold medallion, given by Sir John Astley, M.P.

After further successes at the Agricultural Hall in 1880 and at the Marble Rink, Clapham, in 1881, when he covered 286 miles in 62½ hours, he became the outright winner of the belt. It is now in the Cambridge Folk Museum

**121** Professor J. S. Henslow, Professor of Botany, 1859. He became professor in 1825, and was the first to organise practical work for students on scientific lines. Had there been no Henslow at Cambridge, there might have been no Darwin. For many years the words HENSLOW COMMON INFORMER could be seen on the wall of Corpus Christi College, an echo of the election of 1825 when Professor Henslow strongly opposed the bribery then rampant

**122** Charles Henry Cooper, 1859. He was appointed Town Clerk of Cambridge in 1849 and died in 1866. His monumental books about the history of his adopted town are one of the principal sources of information about the city's past